CREEPY, KOOKY SCIENCE

# Peculiar Places

Eileen Lucas

Enslow Publishing
101 W. 23rd Street
Suite 240
New York, NY 10011
USA
enslow.com

Published in 2020 by Enslow Publishing, LLC.
101 W. 23rd Street, Suite 240, New York, NY 10011

Copyright © 2020 by Enslow Publishing, LLC
All rights reserved.

No part of this book may be reproduced by any means without the written permission of the publisher.

**Library of Congress Cataloging-in-Publication Data**

Names: Lucas, Eileen, author.
Title: Peculiar places / Eileen Lucas.
Description: New York : Enslow Publishing, 2020. | Series: Creepy, kooky science | Audience: Grades 5 to 8. | Includes bibliographical references and index.
Identifiers: LCCN 2019009515| ISBN 9781978513846 (library bound) | ISBN 9781978513839 (pbk.)
Subjects: LCSH: Geographical myths—Juvenile literature. | Geography—Miscellanea—Juvenile literature. | Curiosities and wonders—Juvenile literature.
Classification: LCC GR940 .L83 2020 | DDC 001.94—dc23
LC record available at https://lccn.loc.gov/2019009515

Printed in the United States of America

**To Our Readers**: We have done our best to make sure all websites in this book were active and appropriate when we went to press. However, the author and the publisher have no control over and assume no liability for the material available on those websites or on any websites they may link to. Any comments or suggestions can be sent by email to customerservice@enslow.com.

**Photo Credits**: Peculiar Places – Photo research by Bruce Donnola

Cover, p. 1 The Perfect/Shutterstock.com; p. 5 Mr Nai/Shutterstock.com; p. 8 Bettmann/Getty Images; p. 10 mark peterson/Corbis Historical/Getty Images; p. 12 Barcroft Media/Getty Images; p. 15 Historical Picture Archive/Corbis Historical/Getty Images; p. 16 Alberto Loyo/Shutterstock.com; p. 18 Fotos593/Shutterstock.com; p. 21 M. Scheja/Shutterstock.com; p. 23 RugliG/Shutterstock.com (upper left); p. 23 Fominayaphoto/Shutterstock.com (upper right); p. 23 Borka Kiss/Shutterstock.com (lower left); p. 23 joojoob27/Shutterstock.com (lower right); p. 26 Reimar/Shutterstock.com; p. 28 WindVector/Shutterstock.com; p. 31 Anatoliy Lukich/Shutterstock.com; pp. 32-33 Jay Ondreicka/Shutterstock.com; p. 37 Alasdair Turner/Aurora/Getty Images; pp. 38-39 George Steinmetz/Corbis Documentary/Getty Images

# Contents

# Introduction

There are many amazing places in this world. Some are so beautiful they take one's breath away. Some are very difficult and dangerous to get to or be around. And some are strange and mysterious.

Over many centuries, people have scratched their heads in wonder about these peculiar places. Long ago, the people of ancient Greece built some amazing structures. Yet they wondered about the remains of palaces and temples built long before their time. They decided that these must have been the work of mythical creatures called cyclops.

In England during the Middle Ages, some people thought the mysterious stone pillars found at Stonehenge must have been built by a race of giants. In the modern world, humans look out into space and wonder if they're alone in the universe. If there are extraterrestrials, are they friendly? Or would they be as dangerous as the most frightening science-fiction movies make them seem? Will people meet them someday? Or, perhaps, did aliens already find Earth, long ago?

Generations of scientists have tried to answer many questions about the world's peculiar places. Where did the debris found on a New Mexico ranch in 1947 come from? Who carved the multi-ton statues with long faces found on Easter Island? And why? What has caused many ships and planes to disappear into the infamous Bermuda Triangle? How come strange-colored spots appear in a particular lake in Canada every summer?

Were the pillars of Stonehenge put in place by an ancient race of giants? Today, archaeologists and other scientists provide answers to many of the questions surrounding the world's most peculiar places.

Scientists of many kinds use evidence to answer these questions. Meteorologists explain how weather affects planes and ships in the Bermuda Triangle. Engineers and oceanographers chime in as well. Geologists and chemists consider the composition of rocks and soil as they figure out the age of artifacts found by archaeologists. Paleomagnetists are scientists who specialize in studying ancient magnetic forces. Geophysicists provide valuable input about the properties of Earth and other planets. These and other scientists work together as mystery solvers.

CHAPTER 1

# Areas of Alien Interest

*Chariots of the Gods* was a book published in 1968. Its author, Erich von Daniken (1935– ), got a lot of people talking about aliens. He wrote that many amazing ancient structures could not have been built by humans. Instead, he said that Earth had been visited by extraterrestrials. In 1973, von Daniken's book was followed up with a TV documentary called *In Search of Ancient Astronauts*.

According to the results of a poll released in 2017, about half of all Americans believe that aliens exist.[1] Similar results have been found in polls of citizens of other nations as well. Some scientists also believe in extraterrestrial life, or at least the possibility of it. Silvano P. Colombano works at the Ames National Aeronautics and Space Administration (NASA) Research Center in California.

In 2019, he stated that scientists should at least take seriously the notion that aliens may have visited Earth at some time.[2]

In the 1960s and 1970s, Carl Sagan (1934–1996) considered the possibility of alien life coming to Earth. Sagan was the director of the Laboratory for Planetary Studies at Cornell University. In his book *Intelligent Life in the Universe*, he suggested that extra-terrestrials might want to convert Earthlings to their religion. Or, they might want to crush humans so they, the aliens, would remain superior. Another scientist wondered if maybe aliens would visit Earth to keep humanity from destroying itself![3]

No hard evidence (at least not so far as the public is aware) has ever proven that Earth has, in fact, been visited by aliens. There are an endless number of theories, however. And plenty of peculiar places that still raise questions.

## Roswell, New Mexico

In July 1947, some wreckage was found on a hot and dusty ranch in New Mexico. W. W. Brazel, known as "Mac," couldn't tell what the debris was from. He showed it to the sheriff in the closest town, Roswell. The sheriff called the nearby US Army Air Force base. Word got out, and the newspapers declared that the air force had captured a flying saucer. Quickly, the air force reported that the wreckage was just that of an ordinary weather balloon that had crashed.

US Air Force officers examine and try to identify fragments from a crash near Roswell, New Mexico, in 1947. Some people still wonder where the debris really came from.

Over the following years, a number of unidentified flying object (UFO) sightings were reported throughout the United States and in other parts of the world. These were the years of the Cold War between the United States and the Soviet Union. The governments of each country worried the other might be planning to attack them. UFO reports added to the fears of people everywhere.

From time to time, people would talk about "the Roswell incident" and wonder about the truth of what happened there. In 1995, the US government revealed what it said was "the true identity" of the Roswell debris. It had actually been from a failed Cold War mission to spy on the Soviet Union, the government claimed.[4]

For some people, the matter was settled. For others, the search for answers went on. Some ufologists, or people who study UFOs, claim that an alien spaceship was recovered from Roswell. Groups such as the International Space Sciences Organization (ISSO) and the Search for Extraterrestrial Intelligence Institute (SETI) still search for answers from outer space.

In the meantime, the people of Roswell, New Mexico, have made the most of the public's interest in what happened there. Tiny containers of dirt from the ranch where the debris was found have been packaged and sold to tourists. Each year in July, the town hosts the huge UFO Festival "to commemorate" and celebrate the Roswell incident.[5]

## Area 51

Many people wonder if the public will ever really know what happened at Roswell. Some ufologists believe the answers are locked up in a place known as Area 51.

Area 51 is in a remote part of the Nevada desert. So little is known about it that the *New York Times* once called it "a base so secret it doesn't exist."[6] Some people believe live aliens, or perhaps by now the corpses of aliens, are there! The US Air Force officially calls it the Air Force Flight Test Center, Detachment 3. Officials say it is an airfield that is carefully guarded because it is used for testing top-secret military aircraft. The US Central Intelligence Agency (CIA)

Commonly known as Area 51, this remote part of the Nevada Test and Training Range is highly restricted and carefully guarded. The US government says little about exactly what goes on there.

protects the location and anything that takes place there. Little is known about exactly what activities those might be.

Just outside the boundaries of Area 51 lies the tiny town of Rachel, Nevada. Sometimes referred to as "the UFO capital of the world," the town has only approximately fifty residents. Lots of visitors pass through town along Route 375, nicknamed the "Extraterrestrial Highway." Many of the visitors are likely hoping for some sort of alien encounter.

## Geocaching

Geocaching is an outdoor hobby that uses the Global Positioning System (GPS). Geocachers, people who participate in this hobby, place a small object (the cache) in a particular location. After they report the coordinates of that location, other geocachers may choose to use their GPS to find it. If they do, they report that in a notebook tucked inside the cache. Then they replace the cache for others to find. Peculiar places seem to be of great interest to geocachers. According to one source, some 1,500 geocaches were reportedly placed along Route 375 near Area 51 in 2011.[7]

## Crop Circles

In addition to sites where UFOs are reported, peculiar places known as crop circles have led some people to believe in extraterrestrials. Crop circles are patterns that appear suddenly and mysteriously in farmers' fields, usually overnight. They are most often reported in Great Britain, but they can appear in other places as well.

Crop circles first started being regularly reported in the 1970s. Since then, the study of them has drawn a great deal of interest. It

This crop circle was discovered in a farm field near Wiltshire, England, in July 2013. Its complex pattern shows the detailed design many such circles are known for.

even has its own name: cerology. The name comes from the Roman goddess of agriculture, Ceres. The circles always seem to form in farm fields.

In July 1996, an extremely complex crop circle appeared in the English countryside. It happened to be just across a highway from the archaeological site known as Stonehenge. This crop circle was surprising in several ways. It included a very complicated pattern within the circle. And, it appeared during the daytime, not overnight like most of the others. Evidence suggests that human tricksters, or hoaxers, were behind this crop circle, as well as others.

It might seem that it would be difficult for hoaxers to get in and out of farm fields unnoticed. A number of admitted crop-circle-makers say that it is not. They've developed techniques with simple tools that can fool even the experts. Such tools might include a rope tied to something for support, and a board, perhaps attached to the tricksters' feet, to flatten down crops.

Today, even most cerologists admit that the majority of crop circles are hoaxes. A small percentage, however, seem to defy scientific explanation. They represent a mystery yet to be solved.

CHAPTER 2

# Amazing Ancient Sites

Erich von Daniken isn't the only person to doubt that ancient people could build the amazing structures discovered in their territories. However, scientific evidence now supports the belief that indeed they could, and they did.

## Stonehenge, England

Researchers have been puzzled by the massive stone circle known as Stonehenge in southwestern England for centuries. Who built it, when, and why? In the seventeenth and eighteenth centuries, archaeologists thought that it was a temple used by Celtic druids. This belief was widely held for many years.

Archaeologists continue to gather evidence about the ancient people who lived in this place. The large stones of

## Plain of Jars, Laos

The Plain of Jars is located in Laos, in Southeast Asia. Thousands of stone jars lie scattered in groups across a large plateau. Archaeologists believe they were made some time between 500 BCE and 500 CE. It appears that the jars were most likely part of ancient burial ceremonies.

The Hmong people of Laos tell of a handsome man and his beautiful wife, Ngao Njua.[1] The king of a far-away country wanted her for himself, so he stole her away. Ngao Njua was so unhappy that for three years, the sun did not shine. When her husband finally found her, however, she laughed, and the sun came out and shone brightly. She and her husband escaped, leaving behind many things, which are now seen on the Plain of Jars.

the outer circle were probably put in place between 2600 BCE and 2400 BCE. These hard, sandstone pillars, called sarsen, each weigh about 35 tons (32 metric tons). Somehow, the ancient people transported them to Stonehenge from a site 18 miles (30 kilometers) away. On top of the sarsens sat large flat stones called lintels, which connected the pillars in a ring.

Inside this outer ring of stone are smaller pillars made of spotted dolerite. These pillars, called the bluestones, originally came from southwestern Wales, some 150 miles (241 km) away. That is the only place on Earth where the spotted dolerite is found.

Archaeologist Mike Parker Pearson studied a place called Woodhenge, about 1 mile (1.6 km) away from the stone ring. There, Pearson found evidence of huge feasts that took place long ago. These feasts were likely held when the people gathered for winter

This artwork illustrates a druid ceremony supposed to have taken place at Stonehenge in ancient times. Modern archaeologists continue to piece together evidence of life in the British Isles thousands of years ago.

and summer solstices. They would have seen the rising and setting of the sun in specific places around the stone pillars. Parts of the area were probably reserved for religious ceremonies in addition to those honoring the solstices.[2]

Scientists continue to work on the mysteries of Stonehenge. But the fact that humans lived and died there, and respected and took note of the changing skies and seasons, can be considered proven.

## Easter Island, South Pacific Ocean

An island called Rapa Nui by native people lies more than 2,000 miles (3,219 km) west of South America in the Pacific Ocean. Today, the land is rocky and very little grows there. But it was once a tree-covered tropical paradise. The people who lived there then, and now, are known as Polynesians. Their ancestors likely left Asia in many small boats long, long ago. Those who settled on Rapa Nui in the years between 700 and 1000 planted seeds and developed a rich culture. Over time, they built huge stone altars, called *ahu*, along the shore. These altars probably helped the Polynesians mark and honor the seasons and the passage of time.

For many years, researchers have questioned the purpose and technology behind the huge stone statues of Easter Island, far out in the Pacific Ocean. Some answers have been found, but not all.

Sometime around the year 1000, the island people began creating huge stone statues, called *moai*. Some *moai* sat on *ahu*, but not all. Polynesian legends call the statues *aringa ora*, which means "living faces." They are said to represent important families' ancestors.[3] Their height is between 18 and 23 feet (5.5 to 7 m) tall!

According to archaelogists, *moai* carving stopped suddenly around 1650. Nearly four hundred statues were left unfinished in the quarry. A Dutch ship landed on the island on Easter Sunday, 1722, and gave it the name Easter Island. Much of what had made the island a paradise in the past was gone. The people were hungry and fighting among themselves.

The Dutch did not stay long. But they were followed by other European travelers. These did not find conditions any better for the islanders. Many Polynesians had died of various causes, and the few that remained knew little of the secrets of the mysterious *moai*. Scientists continue to study the island today, searching for clues to the untold story of the long-faced statues.

## Nazca Lines, Peru

A peculiar collection of lines and drawings, called the geoglyphs, was discovered when planes began flying over the Peruvian desert in 1927. The markings from a time long past had remained hidden because they could only be seen in their entirety from the air.

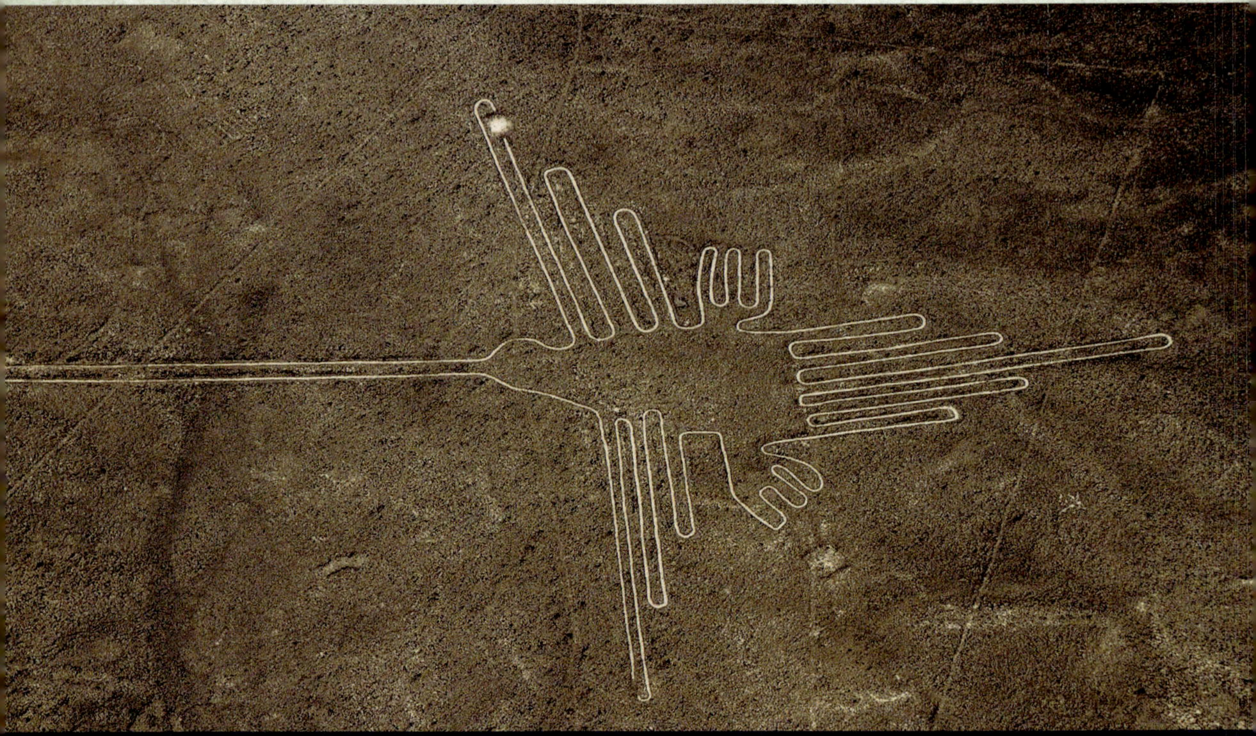

The hummingbird is one of the images that make up the Nazca Lines of Peru. This picture was taken from the air, the only way many of the ancient drawings can be viewed in their entirety.

The drawings are known today as the Nazca (or Nasca) Lines. They are named for a nearby town and for a native people who lived in the area between 200 and 600 CE. More than three hundred drawings have been found, including various shapes as well as figures of humans and animals. In addition, more than eight hundred long, straight lines cross the landscape. These lines are remarkable for their mathematical precision. The people who made them would not have been able to see the complete line, and yet they are extremely straight over long distances!

Some people (such as von Daniken) believed the humanlike figures among the drawings represented alien visitors. The fact that some drawings look like flying-saucer-shaped landing sites added to the mystery. Most archaeologists today believe the pre-Inca Nazca people made the markings.

There are still various theories as to why, however. Archaeologists Paul Kosok and Maria Reiche believed the Nazca people had a special connection with astronomy and agriculture. They would have looked to the sky for guidance on when to plant seeds, harvest, and prepare the soil for the next season.

Some researchers, such as Johan Reinhard in the 1970s, explained that the lines were not a kind of calendar but were made to worship gods. According to this theory, the lines were sacred pathways leading to places where the gods could be honored. Offerings to the gods might also have been made at various places along the journey. Or, some researchers suggest, the drawings themselves were meant as offerings to the gods.[4]

Scientists continue to puzzle over the mystery of the lines and drawings. Meanwhile, the United Nations Educational, Scientific and Cultural Organization (UNESCO) has designated the area as a World Heritage Site.

CHAPTER 3

# Regions of Rainbow Colors

From the brilliant blues of the oceans to the rich greens of grasslands and rain forests, the planet Earth is a colorful place. Even rocks and soil can be multi-hued. Minerals found in nature have been gathered and used as paints. In some places, the land itself appears to be a work of art.

Much of the time, these colors are due to a process called oxidation. This is the same process that takes place when a piece of metal is left out in the rain and a red layer of rust forms on it. There are times when oxidation produces other colors, such as brown or yellow. Green coloring can result when some clays oxidize.

## Rainbow Mountains, Peru and China

Vinicunca is a mountain found in the Andes of Peru. It is also known as La Montaña de Siete Colores (Mountain of Seven Colors). The

**The power of wind and rain wearing away the minerals found in Earth's surface created this colorful landscape in the Rainbow Mountains of the Gansu province in China.**

colors formed with the melting of huge sheets of ice that once covered the area. As the ice melted, water mixed with minerals in the ground. Over time, chemical processes changed the color of the rocks and soil. Red, yellow, even purple and green came from the different minerals found there.

There are also the Rainbow Mountains in the Eastern Hemisphere, in a national park in the northwest of China. Geologists explain that the colors come from iron and other minerals deposited in the sandy soil. Millions of years ago, several pieces of Earth's crust, called plates, collided and folded into each other. This is how the Rainbow Mountains and many other landforms developed. Wind and rain wore down the surface layers of rock in the process called erosion. Water moving through the grains of sand and rock left some minerals behind and washed others away. These minerals are responsible for the striking colors.

## Colorful Beaches

In many parts of the world, the phrase "a sandy beach" brings to mind various shades of white and brown. Some beaches, however, come in surprising colors. They may be midnight black. Others may glitter and shine with a rainbow of colors.

Sand is generally formed by the erosion of rock. As rock is exposed to rain, wind, and freezing and melting snow, particles break off and wash away. Most light-colored beaches are made of bits of eroded quartz, but that depends on what the rocks or cliffs surrounding a beach are made of.

Papakolea Beach in Hawaii is known for its beautiful green sand. The color comes from a mineral called olivine, deposited many years ago by an ancient volcano. Magma from volcanoes is rich in olivine, and it's often one of the first crystals to form as lava cools after a

### Candy Cane Mountain, Azerbaijan

The Caucasus Mountains run through several countries in western Asia, to the north and east of Turkey. Nestled within the Caucasus in the country of Azerbaijan is a place called the Candy Cane Mountains. Travel writer Mark Elliott gave this area its picturesque name.[1] The mixture of pink and white stripes make it look almost good enough to eat! The Candy Cane Mountains won't satisfy a sweet tooth, however. The color is the result of iron oxidation.

Like the Rainbow Mountains, colorful beaches are found in a number of places around the world as a result of erosion and the exposure of minerals in rocks: (*top left*) green sand on Papakolea Beach in Hawaii; (*top right*) black sand on Punalu'u Beach in Hawaii; (*bottom left*) pink sand on Harbour Island in the Bahamas; and (*bottom right*) purple sand on Pfeiffer Beach in California.

volcano erupts. Olivine crystals are heavy, which helps them pile up on a beach and not be washed away by the tide.

Hawaii's Punalu'u Beach is known for its black sand. This color is due to the large amounts of basalt, a rock formed when lava cools quickly. At Punalu'u, magma oozes up from underwater vents, cooling rapidly when it comes into contact with ocean water. This creates fine shards of black basalt that line the beach.

Off the Atlantic coast of North America in the Bahamas is a 3-mile- (5-km-) long beach of pink sand. This beach gets its color from tiny marine organisms. These tiny lifeforms' red shells mix with the beach's white sand, creating the unusual pink color.

Meanwhile, on the western coast of the United States, Pfeiffer Beach in California surprises visitors with its deep violet sand. The color comes from manganese garnet deposits in the surrounding hills. The manganese garnet washes downstream from the hills to the beach. The brightest purples are generally found after winter storms, which help speed the process of erosion.[2]

## Painted Hills, Oregon, and Painted Desert, Arizona

The Painted Hills of Oregon provide a record of changes over millions of years in the northwestern part of North America. Botanists and zoologists join other scientists who come to the region to "read" the record left in the fossils of prehistoric plants and animals. These fossils are found among the stripes of red, yellow, orange, and black of the hills.

In the southwestern part of North America, the Painted Desert is found on the outskirts of the Grand Canyon and within the Petrified Forest National Park. Spanish explorer Francisco Vázquez de Coronado (1510–1554) found the Painted Desert in 1540. He named the area El Desierto Pintado. He'd been searching for a city of gold, but instead he found a palette of colors. This included the common red rock found in many places, as well as more unique shades of lilac and lavender. The colors are the result of multiple layers of limestone, shale, mudstone, and siltstone, which contain large mineral deposits. The forces of oxidation and erosion produce and reveal the colors over many years. Wind is another force that plays a part. It changes the face of the landscape by shifting soil and exposing new layers.

## Spotted Lake, Canada

Sometimes Earth is even painted in what looks like polka dots! In winter and spring, Spotted Lake in British Columbia, Canada, looks just like any other body of water. But when most of the water evaporates in the dry summer months, many giant-sized pools appear within the lake. This creates a landscape speckled with colors of yellow, green, and blue.

The colorful pools are caused by high levels of various minerals and salts collecting in the lake. These minerals include calcium, sodium sulfates, and magnesium sulfate, as well as salts, all eroded from nearby hills. The colors of the pools depend on the

**Minerals and salts left behind after much of the water evaporates is the scientific reason for the polka dot pools of Canada's Spotted Lake. Some people think it looks like a Dr. Seuss creation!**

concentration of minerals in each spot. The magnesium sulfate crystallizes to form a hard surface around and between the spots.[3]

The lake has long been considered a sacred place by native peoples. They used the mud and waters of the lake to heal aches and illnesses. In October 2001, the First Nations and the Indian Affairs Department of Canada purchased the land where the lake is found to protect it.[4]

CHAPTER 4

# Freaky Forces at Sea and on Land

Blowing winds, evaporating waters, and erupting volcanoes have created interesting places on the planet. Other forces of nature and scientific processes can also play a part. Earth's magnetism, the processes of freezing and melting, and mysterious fires can also create strange environments.

## Bermuda Triangle, Atlantic Ocean

Probably among the most famous peculiar places on Earth is an area known as the Bermuda Triangle. It is located in the Atlantic Ocean, roughly between the islands of Bermuda and Puerto Rico, and the state of Florida on the southeast coast of the United States. Many strange things have happened in this area, including thousands of disappearances. For example, in 1880, a British ship,

**There are a number of different ways to outline the region known as the Bermuda Triangle, a mysterious area of the Atlantic Ocean. This map shows the most common.**

HMS *Atalanta*, set sail from Bermuda, headed for England. It never docked, and neither it nor any of the more than three hundred crew members on board were ever found. In 1918, the USS *Cyclops* and its crew of 309 went missing after leaving Barbados. The ship had a radio on board, but no emergency message was received. In 1945, a team of bomber planes, known as Flight 19, went missing during a training flight. The commander of the five planes and fourteen men reported that his team appeared to be off course over the ocean. A seaplane sent out to search for the team also disappeared without a trace.[1] In 1963, the crew of a Boeing 707 reported a strange "frothing" in the sea below them after takeoff from San Juan, Puerto Rico. They said it lasted only about thirty seconds, but it covered about 0.5 miles (1 kilometer) and reached more than 2,000 feet (610 m) into the air![2]

A 1964 magazine article written by a man named Vincent Gaddis gave the area its famous name. He suggested that the missing ships, planes, and people may have disappeared through a black hole–like gateway. Time warps, UFOs, and underwater pyramids are among the many reasons offered by other people for the disappearances.

Most scientists believe that disappearances in this area are most likely due to natural, though perhaps peculiar, occurrences. The treacherous currents of the Gulf Stream in the Atlantic Ocean are capable of carrying away wreckage from accidents. The US Coast Guard explains that raging storms, strong currents, waterspouts (tornadoes that suck up water from the sea), and mysterious forces yet to be understood likely play a role in the disappearances that happen there.

One of the forces that scientists don't yet have all the answers to is electromagnetism and other kinds of energy that surround and make up Earth. This could have something to do with the strange compass readings sea captains and pilots have reported in the area of the Bermuda Triangle. Another is the possibility of a form of methane gas rising up in bursts from the ocean floor and creating disturbances on the surface. It's these and other "forces yet to be understood" that keep many people scratching their heads about this perhaps dangerous, peculiar place.

## The Traveling Stones of Death Valley, California

Death Valley National Park is located in California. The lowest point in the United States is located here in Badwater Basin. The difference between that and the highest point in Death Valley, Telescope Peak, just a few miles away, is more than 2 miles (3 km). That's two times the depth of the Grand Canyon![3]

Arguably one of the most peculiar parts of Death Valley is a place called Racetrack Playa, where the Traveling Stones are found. (They are also sometimes called the Sailing Stones.) Rocks of all sizes, from a few ounces to hundreds of pounds, move across the ground without any visible cause.

The rocks of Racetrack Playa tumble down from the nearby mountains. Once they come to rest on the desert surface, however, they somehow move along the ground. No one has actually

After rainwater evaporates in the dried-up lake bed in Death Valley, California, it leaves a surface of slick mud and then a pattern of cracks, as well as the trails of the Traveling Stones.

witnessed them move, but they leave trails behind them as evidence. Some of these trails have been as long as 1,500 feet (457 m)![4]

In 2014, scientists "spied" on the rocks with time-lapse photography.[5] This provided evidence of the forces that cause the stones to move: ice, water, and wind. Sometimes rainfall followed by heavy winds cause the rocks to sail along the slickened mud. During the winter, rain that falls during the day can freeze into a solid sheet of ice at night. As the ice sheet breaks apart in the heat of the day, chunks gather behind stones that became frozen in the ice. Then wind along with the melting ice force the stones forward, bit by bit. Repeated over and over, these processes account for the Traveling Stones of Racetrack Playa.

## Eternal Flame Falls, New York State

A small waterfall in western New York State attracts many visitors to see the flame that burns behind the water. The mystery of Eternal Flame Falls was solved when geologists studied the natural gas leak located there. They determined that the natural gas leaks out from deposits deep within Earth, opened along fault lines. The gas is always there, waiting for a spark to ignite it.

Occasionally the flame does go out. Then, hikers passing by relight it. Eternal Flame Falls is not the only flame caused by a natural gas pocket. However, the image of a single flame under a rushing waterfall does make it rather unique.

The mysterious flame that burns almost continuously can be seen amidst the rocks and behind the falling waters of Eternal Flame Falls, near Buffalo, New York.

## Burning Mountain, Australia

For more than five thousand years, a fire has been burning just below ground in the mountains of New South Wales, Australia. No one knows for sure exactly how the fire started. The Aboriginal people of Australia told of the fiery tears of a woman who was turned to stone. Another story says that a man who was trying to start a fire was dragged under the ground by evil spirits. The smoke from the fire is the man warning others to stay away.

A more likely cause for the fire's start is a lightning strike. Scientists do know that the reason the fire keeps burning is that it started at the site of a large underground seam of coal. There are other places in the world where coal seams burn underground. According to one report, there may be more than a thousand burning around the world at any time. They don't often become big news, however, because they are put out within a few days or weeks.

Mount Wingen, popularly known as Burning Mountain, is another story. It is the oldest continuous coal fire in the world. It is located about 140 miles (224 km) north of Sydney. The fire burns continuously about 90 feet (30 m) below the ground. It has been moving southward as it burns at the very slow rate of about 3 feet (1 meter) per year. In its wake, it has left a trail of devastation where no plant life grows.[6]

CHAPTER 5

# Other Wonderfully Weird Places

A blood-red river surrounded by the pure white of an Antarctic glacier is certainly a peculiar place. Most people would find this destination a seriously creepy one as well. Meanwhile, in the Siberian wilderness at the opposite end of Earth, an "alley" marked off by giant whale bones presents another creepy sight. Close to the central latitudes of the planet, visitors to Lake Natron in Tanzania may be creeped out by perfectly preserved dead animals petrified in the lake's poisonous waters.

A more pleasant place is found in the Indian Ocean. In the waters surrounding the Island of Vadhoo, magically peculiar lights shine in the dark.

## Blood Falls, Antarctica

The entire continent of Antarctica might easily be considered a pretty peculiar place, and a dangerous one. There's a reason why Antarctica is the only continent without any indigenous people of its own!

Still, brave explorers and sturdy scientists have shed blood, sweat, and tears studying the frozen glaciers that cover the land. Speaking of blood, in 1911 a geologist reported seeing a river that was blood red in color on Antarctica's Taylor Glacier. The river flowed over a cliff that was stained with the same dark red color. Realizing, of course, that it wasn't really blood, scientists at first thought the color might be the result of a form of algae in the river.

Scientists now know that the red color is caused by oxidized iron in the water. In other words, the river is rusty. They used a technique called radio-echo sounding (RES) to see what was under Taylor Glacier.[1] They found that the water in the river was made up of a brine solution, commonly known as saltwater. This was in contrast to the "fresh," non-salty ice of the glacier. The river water came from a saltwater lake buried deep underneath Taylor Glacier. Over time, the brine made its way up through channels and openings in the glacier. Along the way, it picked up iron from the bedrock. The research team calculated that it took the brine water approximately 1.5 million years to make its way to Blood Falls.[2]

Salty water from a lake buried deep under Taylor Glacier picks up iron as it slowly seeps upward, creating the red coloring of Blood Falls, Antarctica.

## Whale Bone Alley, Siberia

In 1976, Soviet archaeologists discovered a mysterious structure on an island off the coast of Siberia. Two rows of whale bones outlined a very peculiar road. The alley of bones along the shore of Yttygran Island has become known as Whale Bone Alley. Some archaeologists call it "Siberia's slightly creepier answer to Stonehenge."[3] Scientific testing has revealed that the alley is made up of six-hundred-year-old whale jaw and rib bones. They are propped up by rocks in the snow.

The site was likely a sacred meeting place for the indigenous people, known as the Yupik, who hunted whales for food. Square pits in the middle of Whale Bone Alley could have been filled with mounds of meat during feasts and celebrations.

## Lake Natron, Tanzania

Natron is a mixture of salt and minerals found in volcanic ash. It is also the name of a lake located in the African nation of Tanzania. Lake Natron is fed by spring water that is rich in minerals. The minerals make the lake highly alkaline, with a pH of 9 to 10.5. (By comparison, seawater has a pH between about 7 and 9.) As if the alkalinity isn't bad enough, the temperature of Lake Natron water can reach 140 degrees Fahrenheit (60 degrees Celsius).[4]

All of this makes Lake Natron a very deadly place. What makes it an extra creepy place is the fact that animals that die in the lake are turned into statues. This happens through a process called calcification. The

The hot, salty water of Lake Natron in the Great Rift Valley of Africa is a generally hostile environment. One exception is a kind of algae that loves the salt and gives the lake a red color.

extreme sodium bicarbonate content preserves the dead animals. A photographer named Nick Brandt discovered the calcified creatures on a trip to photograph the lake.[5]

A few animal species are actually able to survive in and around the petrifying lake. One species of fish, the alkaline tilapia, lives along the edges. The lake's pink-to-bright-red coloring comes from microorganisms that also love the alkalinity. And the lake is an important breeding ground for a species called lesser flamingos.

## The Sea of Stars, Maldives, Indian Ocean

Among the tropical islands known as the Maldives in the Indian Ocean is one known for an exceptionally beautiful peculiarity. At night, the water lapping the shores of Vadhoo Island appears to be filled with stars.[6]

Scientists have shown that this mysterious phenomenon is actually caused by bioluminescent phytoplankton. Bioluminescence is the ability of an organism to give off light. Phytoplankton are tiny organisms that feed off the sun's energy. A chemical reaction in the phytoplankton off Vadhoo Island produces a fluorescent-looking light.[7] These lights in the water can be seen in a number of other places as well. Another site where it occurs regularly is off the coast of Vieques in the Puerto Rican islands.

Whether easily explained or mystifying, people are fascinated by strange places. Scientists study the movement of ice and wind, and the rain and waves that build up and tear down the surface of Earth. Technology helps other scientists match ancient artifacts with the cultures that left them behind. Over time, scientists piece together the stories behind all the places of the world, from the very common and ordinary to the most unique and peculiar.

# Chapter Notes

## Chapter 1. Areas of Alien Interest


1. Alejandro Rojas, "New Survey Shows Nearly Half of Americans Believe in Aliens," *Huffington Post*, August 2, 2017, https://www.huffingtonpost.com/entry/new-survey-shows-nearly-half-of-americans-believe-in_us_59824c11e4b03d0624b0abe4.
2. Rafi Letzter, "Here's the Truth Behind a NASA Document on Aliens Visiting Earth," Live Science, December 5, 2018, https://www.livescience.com/64237-nasa-aliens-fox-news.html.
3. Norma Gafron, *The Bermuda Triangle* (San Diego, CA: Greenhaven Press, 1995), pp. 87–88.
4. Kathleen Krull, *What Really Happened in Roswell?* (New York, NY: HarperCollins, 2003), p. 36.
5. UFO Festival, Roswell, New Mexico, 2019, http://www.ufofestivalroswell.com/.
6. Ken Karst, *Area 51* (Mankato, MN: Creative Education, 2015), p. 8.
7. Karst, p. 44.


## Chapter 2. Amazing Ancient Sites


1. Adapted from *Zaj Lus: A Hmong Children's Story Collection* (Weston, WI: D. C. Everest Area Schools, 2010).
2. Marc Aronson, *If Stones Could Speak: Unlocking the Secrets of Stonehenge* (Washington, DC: National Geographic Press, 2010), p. 47.
3. Caroline Arnold, *Easter Island: Giant Stone Statues Tell of a Rich and Tragic Past* (New York, NY: Clarion Books, 2000), p. 24.

4. Peter James and Nick Thorpe, *Ancient Mysteries* (New York, NY: Ballantine Books, 1999), pp. 332–336.

## Chapter 3. Regions of Rainbow Colors

1. Mark Elliott, *Azerbaijan: With Excursions to Georgia*, 4th edition (Surrey, UK: Trailblazer Publications, 2010).
2. Natasha Geiling, "The World's Most Colorful Beaches," *Smithsonian*, August 26, 2014, https://www.smithsonianmag.com/travel/worlds-most-colorful-beaches-180952354/.
3. Kaushik, "Spotted Lake, Canada," Amusing Planet, 2019, https://www.amusingplanet.com/2012/01/spotted-lake-canada.html.
4. Mary Jo Dilonardo, "The Mystery of Canada's Magical Spotted Lake," Mother Nature Network, September 21, 2017, https://www.mnn.com/earth-matters/wilderness-resources/blogs/mystery-canada-spotted-lake.

## Chapter 4. Freaky Forces at Sea and on Land

1. "The Mystery of Flight 19," Naval Air Station Fort Lauderdale Museum, https://www.nasflmuseum.com/flight-19.html (accessed April 2, 2019).
2. Chris Oxlade, *The Mystery of the Bermuda Triangle* (Des Plaines, IL: Heinemann Library, 2000), p. 12.
3. Ryan Nagelhout, *How Did Death Valley Get Its Name? And Other FAQs About Geography* (New York, NY: Gareth Stevens, 2017), p. 7.
4. "The Racetrack," National Park Service–Death Valley, September 25, 2016, https://www.nps.gov/deva/planyourvisit/the-racetrack.htm.
5. "The Sailing Stones of Death Valley," National Park Foundation, February 9, 2016, https://www.nationalparks.org/connect/blog/sailing-stones-death-valley.

6. "Burning Mountain: 6000-year-old Coal Fire Moves One Meter Per Year," Atlas Obscura, 2019, https://www.atlasobscura.com/places/burning-mountain; "Burning Mountain Nature Reserve," National Parks NSW, 2019, https://www.nationalparks.nsw.gov.au/visit-a-park/parks/burning-mountain-nature-reserve.

## Chapter 5. Other Wonderfully Weird Places

1. Trevor Nace, "Mystery of Antarctica's Blood Falls Is Finally Solved," Forbes: Science, April 28, 2017, https://www.forbes.com/sites/trevornace/2017/04/28/mystery-of-antarcticas-blood-falls-is-finally-solved/#257a15e12ef8.
2. Sankalan Baidya, "30 Interesting Blood Falls Facts," Facts Legend, September 4, 2015, https://factslegend.org/30-interesting-blood-falls-facts-a-glacier-that-bleeds/.
3. Fiona MacDonald, "Welcome to Whale Bone Alley: Siberia's Eerie Answer to Stonehenge," Science Alert, December 3, 2014, https://www.sciencealert.com/welcome-to-whale-bone-alley-siberia-s-eerie-answer-to-stonehenge.
4. "Lake Natron, Tanzania," NASA Earth Observatory, https://earthobservatory.nasa.gov/images/5465/lake-natron-tanzania (accessed April 2, 2019).
5. Rowan Hooper, "Deadly Lake Turns Animals into Statues," *New Scientist*, September 25, 2013, https://www.newscientist.com/article/mg21929360-100-deadly-lake-turns-animals-into-statues/.
6. Sana Lane, "Sea of Stars: Vadhoo Island (Maldives)," Fiboni, April 18, 2013, http://www.fiboni.com/2013/04/sea-of-stars-vadhoo-island-maldives/.
7. Lane, "Sea of Stars."

# Glossary

**alkaline** Having a pH of greater than 7; in comparison, acids have a pH of less than 7.

**bioluminescence** Light produced by living creatures.

**calcification** A process that adds calcium or calcium salts to the surface of something, thereby hardening that surface.

**coordinates** Two numbers, the intersection of which marks a point on a plane. Numbers associated with latitude and longitude are examples of coordinates used to locate a specific place on Earth.

**electromagnetism** An attraction between objects made of iron or steel, specifically related to electric currents.

**erosion** The process of wearing or grinding down, as by water and wind.

**extraterrestrial** Having to do with life or objects beyond Earth.

**geocaching** An activity that uses the Global Positioning System (GPS) to locate and direct others to specific coordinates. At that location, the participants, called geocachers, will find a cache, a small object that has been placed there for them to find.

**geoglyph** A drawing or marking made on the ground.

**hoax** A trick, often intended to fool someone without them knowing it's a trick.

**indigenous** Native to a place.

**magma** Melted rock between Earth's crust and its core.

**methane** A colorless and odorless gas found naturally in the earth, often used as a fuel.

**microorganism** A tiny living thing, often made up of only one cell and generally visible only under a microscope.

**oxidation** The chemical process in which oxygen is added to another substance.

**pH** A number assigned from 0 to 14 that tells how acidic or alkaline a substance is. Acids, such as battery acid or lemon juice, have a pH of 0 to 6. Neutral substances, such as water, have a pH of 7. Alkaline substances, such as baking soda or bleach, have a pH of 8 to 14.

**phytoplankton** Extremely tiny marine organisms.

**solstice** The event that happens two times each year (winter and summer) as the sun reaches its closest and farthest points from Earth's equator.

# Further Reading

## Books

Hengel, Katherine. *Cool Maps & Geocaching*. North Mankato, MN: ABDO Publishing, 2016.

Manzanero, Paula. *Where Is Area 51?* New York, NY: Penguin Workshop, 2018.

Nagelhout, Ryan. *How Did Death Valley Get Its Name? And Other FAQs About Geography*. New York, NY: Gareth Stevens, 2017.

Omoth, Tyler. *Handbook to Stonehenge, the Bermuda Triangle, and Other Mysterious Locations*. North Mankato, MN: Capstone Press, 2017.

## Websites

**English Heritage: Stonehenge**
*www.english-heritage.org.uk/visit/places/stonehenge/*
Learn more about one of England's most famous sites.

**History: Roswell**
*www.history.com/topics/paranormal/roswell*
Explore the facts and theories behind the Roswell incident.

**National Geographic: Nazca Lines**
*www.nationalgeographic.com/archaeology-and-history/archaeology/nasca-lines/*
Dive deeper into the mystery of Peru's Nazca Lines.

# Index